Claiming Light and Darkness

poems by

Sally Witt

Finishing Line Press
Georgetown, Kentucky

Claiming Light and Darkness

ACKNOWLEDGMENTS

Thanks to *Delta Epsilon Sigma Journal* for permission to use "Row Houses in Winter" (Vol. XXXII no. 1, Mar. 1987) and "No One Told" [published as "Untitled" (Vol. XXXII no. 2, Oct. 1987)]

Other poems published here have appeared in:

The Kith Review, Cinnamon Press, Autumn 2022—"Wings of Stillness"
Spirituality, Dominican journal, Dublin, Ireland—"Autumn Sunset," Vol. 26, September/October 2020
Nuances, literary and art magazine of La Roche College (now University)—"Winter Solstice," 1998
The Loyalhanna Review, literary magazine of Ligonier Valley Writers—"Mountain in April," 2014; "Little Tree in the Town of Lilly" (published as "Small Tree in Lilly, PA"), 2014; "Route 79 North in Winter," 2015; "Trees Lining Washington Street," 2018; "Words to Some Sudden Rays of Sun," 2019; "Demolition of a Steel Products Mill in Ambridge," 2021
The Garden Quarto, Spring 2023, "To a White Butterfly in a Garden" (printed with revisions).

Publisher: Leah Huete de Maines
Editor: Christen Kincaid
Cover Art: Gerrie Grandpre
Author Photo: Gerrie Grandpre
Cover Design: Elizabeth Maines McCleavy

Order online: www.finishinglinepress.com
also available on amazon.com

Author inquiries and mail orders:
Finishing Line Press
PO Box 1626
Georgetown, Kentucky 40324
USA

Contents

In memory of Sr. Mary Catherine Vukmanic, OSU, who taught at Ursuline Academy in Pittsburgh in my grade school years and is the first poet I ever knew

Introduction

All of us search for light, and the presence of darkness in our lives urges us to seek it again and again. We desire light so intensely that we can experience its absence as a deprivation.

But aren't darkness and light both part of our lives and our world? Don't they both, in some way, belong to us? Imagine, for example, repeated days of brightness with never any calming rest of nighttime. Each time of day and each angle of the sun hold a particular gift that no other hour can offer.

These poems represent an attempt to claim both dark and light. They begin in winter, the darkest season in the northern hemisphere. They move into lighter seasons, then return to times of waning light. But their real work is to seek the wealth of light in the darkest times, and to provide space for the richness of night in periods of abundant sun.

Winter Solstice

After equinox,
one hemisphere
stretches into darkness,

finds there what it forgot from ancient turning:
that dark is frightening,
   lonely,
   holy,

and in its deepest, longest hour,
one who dwells in it
may learn where light is born.

Sunset on December 20

O evening sun,
when you disappear behind the mountain,
remember me.

Darkness
knows me well
already.

Winter's Light

Winter's light
comes suddenly.

It leaps from hills
when bare trees' lacy shadows
grace fresh snow.

It breaks through pearl-gray clouds,
to cast a sudden ray of sun
upon a heart forgetful
of the feel of silent warmth.

O silent warmth,
O silent, strengthening warmth,
you have found a way
to my forgetting heart.

Come. This moment
break into the forgetting heart
of this whole wintered, wanting world.

Melt the frozen blindness
concealing patient light,
aglow, despite denial,
deep within our winter hearts.

Row Houses in Winter

When day draws heavily toward dark,
when air is misty damp and smoke,
houses huddle closer than in lighter seasons.

Who offers warmth to them?
Who would give them light
without computing costs and mailing bills?

Who would guess
those homes have hearts?

In February

When spring comes,
will it know how February was—

      how the cold of late winter
      bore no olive branch of hope;

      how bare trees silhouetted against the sky
      shunned any hint of life;

      how we went about our daily obligations
      just because we could not think of any other course?

If spring appears with gaudy colors,
looking like a hundred smiley faces,

if it comes with only surface sweetness,
bar its entrance.

But come, dear Spring that knew us in our February,
and kisses into life the dormant longing of our hearts.

Sleet on March 22

A squall of sleet
strikes roofs and metal awnings
as winter proves it has remained with us.

Yes, the equinox of spring occurred,
but this is the first day after.
Winter was unprepared for banishment.
Who can blame it?

Had we really come to know its gifts,
        its invitation into depth,
                to seeking light within?
      Its call to search for strength
                in face of freezing storms?

Come swirl your season's final sleet, dear winter;
our hearts cannot be whole without you.
Yet still, do not be disappointed
when we speak with love
to spring's first tiny crocuses.

To the Early Daffodils

O daffodils,
dear bent-under-snow daffodils,
warm days came early
and called you into flower.

Would that we had warned you,
yet if we had,
what could you have done?
Life had lured you into gaiety just then.

But snow came suddenly,
weighed on your stems,
and pushed your flowers to the ground;
sharp winds pierced your time of blooming.

Yet even now, while cold continues,
you rise cautiously
to greet the sun
that stoops toward you.

Ah, if I could rise
and stretch toward light
that penetrates the burdens
trampling on fragility!

O straightening,
springing daffodils,
you open heaven
with your rising.

Mountain in April

O April Mountain,
you are pure delicacy,
sprung out of winter.

No One Told

No one told the tree
the house it stood before
was vacant, boarded, vandalized.

So it blossomed into spring
then greened to summer
unknowing
   —or, defiant.

A Rainbow in Three Perspectives

Early evening
Yesterday, after early evening rain,
I saw the faint remnant of a rainbow,
and even now I cling to it.

The poorest ones
This is like the time of Noah;
the very earth would cast us off,
seeing us a species of consumption.
O, may it gather in a healing space
the poorest ones,
where they may feast on fullness—
mountains, birds, the oceans, trees—
where they might imbibe the love creation lavished.

Outside the ark
Noah was careful
in declaring life safe outside the ark;
so much was drowned.
An olive leaf called him to come forth,
and God's many-colored arc above told all of them—
animal and human—
            the earth was new
            and longed for them again.

An Incident While Planting

No matter what you think,
it can come upon you suddenly.
Without warning
you find it sitting in your heart
as it if belonged or lived there
and had always been in reaching distance.

For a long while
you could not even have described it,
and certainly were not expecting it.

Still, there within you waits joy,
thrilled with your notice
and your smile in her direction.

Joy—
that breath of God
that catches you
as you plant another flowering annual
or turn to any task so mundane
you never dreamed it mattered.

To a White Butterfly in a Garden

Greetings to you,
white butterfly among the flowers.

Do you know the gardener is dissatisfied?
She wants at least
to bring the three white hydrangeas close together,
adjust the placement of echinacea,
curb nepeta's wild spread.

I must tell her you are here,
and how, in fluttering delight,
you proclaim the blooming of this very day
enough to call forth
deep and prayerful praise.

Wings of Stillness
for the Sisters of St. Joseph of Watertown, NY

Your days combine great works with simple acts
of worship, welcoming the stranger, washing dishes;
fashioning the earth in needle points of color,
you are faithful to a deep, rushing prayer.

So, at the time of day
when the sun turns into liquid brilliance
and drips behind the mountaintops,

when clouds fall into pink and purple layers,
forming beauty after beauty in the changing light,
set aside the book of prayers, the dishpan.
Come to watch magnificence of evening.

This is your prayer translated into color,
your faithful, daily prayer
that runs to God on wings of stillness.

The book and dishpan will return,
but for these sunset minutes
see the longing of your soul
embraced by God.

Trees Lining Washington Street
(as seen from a fourth floor window)

In morning their eastern shadows
reach across
to partners on the other side.

Near noon,
they gather into silence,
shading only what is nearest them.

By early evening,
west extends to east,
again lacing the street in patterns intricate, precise.

After dark they stand alone
incapable of reaching out
or knowing how their strength is built.

When light returns, again they spread protective shade,
as all of us would do
if we were stately, gracious, and rooted deeply.

Words to Some Sudden Rays of Sun

Really, Friends,
>how did you get into
>my summer evening kitchen?

You had to squeeze
>between the clouds that border you,
stoop underneath
>our back porch awning,
slide down the screen door's frame
to fall right there,
>where I would see you
>as I turned
>from baking preparations.

How, really, did you find your way—
more than ninety-two million miles
to this kitchen floor—
>let alone the distance
>from there into my heart,
to say you knew,
more surely than I did,
that something deep within me
longs for light?

After Sunset

There to the west
the sycamore branches float
in the day's last, dimming sunlight,

while pines to the east
have already leaned back
against the night sky.

The pines had nearly forgotten
this, too, is a place of rest,
and though the night is not solely theirs,

they may lie in it
until the dawn
whispers it is coming back.

Morning Prayer
(from a small chapel in the motherhouse of the Sisters of St. Joseph of
Concordia, KS)

Here in the fourth floor chapel
we again discover
the wide Kansas sky
stretching toward morning.

Below, at highway 81,
where fast food lights
never dimmed throughout the night,
the "Place Orders Here" lanes
attract their breakfast seekers.

Here we meet each other—
they from the hurried lanes of life
hungry for a quick new taste of day,
we, given to waiting for light
while stretching out our own worn wonder—

caught together, all of us,
in the undeserved and unexpected wideness
of new, unbounded love.

Autumn Sunset

The lingering rays of western-falling sun
somersaulted over to the eastern mountains,
kissing them good-night.

The leaves that clung to mountain trees,
surprised at tenderness
upon their evening, brittle days,
became aglow,
until the mountains were a moon of sunset.

Then, in darkening hours,
nighttime wind arrived,
severing leaves from branches
that had borne them.

Thrust upon the mountain floor,
the leaves did not resist
the elements that tore them;

they found contentment
knowing they had carried sun
to this dark place.

Cityscape

The maple tree
behind our house
absorbs the autumn morning sun

in such abundance
that it echoes light.
It gleams in bold defiance

of the alley where it stands,
or the steel mill some yards down,
with buildings vacant, land depressed

from years of serving industry.
This day the tree defies
decay, the ending year, the falling.

In hours to come it will take in light
through varied shades of afternoon,
and evening's glancing rays.

At night
it will find nourishment
in light its golden leaves drank earlier,

the light that lives in it
with vibrant stillness
hidden from the morning glow.

Autumn Evening

The early evening rays of sun
snuggle into maple leaves
and play among the pine branches.

Just before the night begins to fall,
the leaves and pine needles, filled with sun,
come to understand its message:

> Do not fear.
> Remember, you are drenched
> indelibly in love.

Grace before dinner

It's five o'clock.
The late November sun
gathers into brightness
every color of this autumn day.

Spreading light through sky and mountains,
the sun extends a final burst of brilliance,
then slips behind the hills,
gone now from our vision.

Evening deepens,
the view around us changes.
Fields, trees that just sang out in light
grow dim and quiet.

It is the dinner hour.
Still held dearly
in this unfolding prayer of grace,
we spread our table.

The evening light has set before our eyes
creation's precious fruit,
and has shown us, too,
the deepest hunger of our hearts.

Gray Clouds

Gray clouds
dull the river's surface.

Gray clouds
obscure the sun and sky,
they leave the river leaden.

Gray clouds impart
their own strange beauty to the river,
for they alone may speak to it in promise:

> You will not be desolate or parched,
> instead, you will be nourisher of life.
> Your thirst will not be fatal,
> we have come to you.

Route 79 North in Winter

When shadows of bare trees—
      strong and certain,
         sometimes intricate as lace—
fall on fields of snow,

doesn't your heart leap
at what the unexpected winter light reveals,
at beauty deeper than death or any darkness!

Demolition of a steel products mill in Ambridge

How long has it been
since sun has touched this ground
where a steel mill stood for decades?

Months ago a fire halted all production.
Now an excavator arm
claws the brick and metal structure.

Beams weaken, fall—
sun squeezes in where machines and chemicals once reigned,
where workers walked in heavy gear.

How many decades ago
did this land last see a spot of sun?
Does the ground remember
when a rush of wind
last brushed its surface?

I pray that soon the neighbors
will see more sky;
that land made foul by constant productivity
may feel the sun's caress this very day;

that all of us
may find release from walls and roofs
demanding unrelenting usefulness,

that with the land beneath this falling building
we may welcome wind's rush and sun's embrace
on all we have ignored
long decades deep within ourselves.

Little Tree in the Town of Lilly

Courage to you, ice-covered tree!
Do you know you are beautiful,
shining even,
as winter weighs on you?

Sally Witt, a Sister of St. Joseph of Baden, Pennsylvania, is a native of Pittsburgh. Although she has lived briefly in Washington, D.C., Watertown, NY, and Concordia, KS, most of her life has been spent in Pittsburgh's neighborhoods and the surrounding industrial towns of the western part of the state.

She is accustomed to skies of industrial places and to land left in the wake of heavy industry. She lives where rivers have been used in the service of profit, and air pollution is common. In these places she has been among people who are hardly aware their ordinary goodness helps to hold the world together.

Her work has been in education from elementary school through college, as well as in the fields of history and communications. She initiated an oral history project for her congregation that included the industrial roots of the sisters, their families and neighbors. She has also written histories of the Sisters of St. Joseph of Watertown, NY (*Sisters of the North Country*, 2005), The Holy Spirit Sisters of Pittsburgh (*A Hidden Spirit*, 2014), and the Sisters of St. Joseph of Concordia, KS (*Beyond the Frontier*, 2020).

Her poetry has appeared in the *Christian Century, Bearings Online, Spirituality, the Kith Review*, and other publications.

www.ingramcontent.com/pod-product-compliance
Lightning Source LLC
Chambersburg PA
CBHW022055080426
42734CB00009B/1357

*9 7 9 8 8 8 8 3 8 5 2 2 7 *